UNITED STATES
the culture

Lynne Weiss

The LanSeries

The Lands, Peoples, and Cultures Series
Created by Bobbie Kalman

Author: Lynne Weiss

Editor: Lynn Peppas

Proofreader: Rachel Eagen

Photo research: Crystal Sikkens, Planman Technologies

Editorial director: Kathy Middleton

Design: Planman Technologies

Production coordinator: Margaret Amy Salter

Prepress technician: Margaret Amy Salter

Print coordinator: Katherine Berti

Written, developed, and produced by Planman Technologies

Cover: Native American Pow Wow dancer

Title page: The Statue of Liberty

Back cover: Bald Eagle

Icon: The Liberty Bell

Illustrations:
Bonna Rouse: back cover
Planman Technologies: p. 23

Photographs:
Dreamstime: p. 13 (b)
Corbis: © Ted Streshinsky: p. 8 (tr)
istockphoto.com: p. 4 (t), 7 (bl)
Keystone Press: © Entertainment Pictures: p. 15 (br); © wenn.com: 27 (bl); U-T San Diego/ZUMApress: 27 (br); Little House, Inc./Entertainment Pictures: 28
Library of Congress: p. 4 (b), 11 (tl), 13 (t), 14 (t), 25 (b)
NASA: p. 29 (t); Photo by FOTOS Intl. /KEYSTONE Canada: 30 (b)
Shutterstock.com: Doug James: front cover; Jason and Bonnie Grower: p. 5 (t); aceshot1: 6; 7 (t), 8 (br), Zurijeta: 9 (t); 10 (t), Jose Gil: 12 (r); 15 (t), Joe Seer: 16 (r); Featureflash: 16 (b), 30 (t); Isabel FernÃ¡ndez FernÃ¡ndez: 18 (l); 19 (b), 20 (t), 20 (t & bl), Evan Meyer: 21 (t); 24, Helga Esteb: 29 (b); 31
Thinkstock.com: title page, p. 3, 5 (b), 7 (br), 8 (bl), 9 (b), 10 (b), 11 (tr & b), 14 (b), 17 (b), 20 (br)
Wikimedia Commons: Apavlo: p. 12 (t); Replytojain:12 (b); United States Department of Defense: 15 (bl); 16 (tl), 17 (t), Ansel Admas/United States Goverment: 18 (r); Finlay McWalter: 19 (t); Carol M Highsmith: 21 (b); Noah Webster: 22 (l); 25 (t), 26 (r), Angela Radulescu: 27 (t)

Every effort has been made to obtain the appropriate credit and full copyright clearance for all images in this book. Any oversights, despite Crabtree's greatest precautions, will be corrected in future editions.

Library and Archives Canada Cataloguing in Publication

Weiss, Lynne
    United States : the culture / Lynne Weiss.

(The lands, peoples, and cultures series)
Includes index.
Issued also in electronic formats.
ISBN 978-0-7787-9834-7 (bound).--ISBN 978-0-7787-9837-8 (pbk.)

    1. United States--Social life and customs--Juvenile literature.
2. United States--Civilization--Juvenile literature. I. Title.
II. Series: Lands, peoples, and cultures series

E161.W44 2012   j973   C2012-902717-0

Library of Congress Cataloging-in-Publication Data

Weiss, Lynne.
    United States the culture / Lynne Weiss.
      p. cm. -- (The lands, peoples, and cultures series)
    Includes an index.
    ISBN 978-0-7787-9834-7 (reinforced library binding : alk. paper) -- ISBN 978-0-7787-9837-8 (pbk. : alk. paper) -- ISBN 978-1-4271-7893-0 (electronic pdf.) -- ISBN 978-1-4271-8008-7 (electronic html.)
    1. United States--Social life and customs--Juvenile literature. 2. United States--Civilization--Juvenile literature. I. Title.

E161.W45 2012
973--dc23
                         2012016096

Crabtree Publishing Company

www.crabtreebooks.com   1-800-387-7650

Printed in Canada/102012/MA20120817

Published in Canada
Crabtree Publishing
616 Welland Ave.
St. Catharines, Ontario
L2M 5V6

Published in the United States
Crabtree Publishing
PMB 59051
350 Fifth Avenue, 59th Floor
New York, New York 10118

Published in the United Kingdom
Crabtree Publishing
Maritime House
Basin Road North, Hove
BN41 1WR

Published in Australia
Crabtree Publishing
3 Charles Street
Coburg North
VIC, 3058

Contents

4   An influential culture

6   Many faiths

8   Celebrating religion

10   Holidays through the year

14   Many styles of music

17   American art

20   American architecture

22   Speaking English

23   American lore and legend

25   The world of literature

29   On screen, big and small

32   Glossary and Index

The culture of the United States is made up of many parts, and it is as diverse as the American people. The culture comes from many aspects of American life, including music, art and architecture, literature, television and movies, religion, and holiday celebrations.

Technology and innovation, new ideas and new ways of doing things, play a major role in American culture, too. The work of American **inventors** has changed the way people all over the world travel, live, and communicate. Wilbur and Orville Wright invented an early airplane. Thomas Edison invented lightbulbs and recorded sound. Alexander Graham Bell experimented with ways to transmit sound, and in 1876 he invented the telephone. In recent years, Grace Hopper developed a way to program computers. American engineers and scientists worked together to send astronauts to the moon, and to create the Internet. Search engines, social networking sites, and e-mail all use the Internet, and it plays a growing role in the changing American society.

The culture of the United States has spread around the world. People in many different countries watch American movies and television series, listen to American music, wear American-designed clothing, and drive cars designed in the United States.

(above) Over the past few years, social networking sites have grown immensely in popularity. Mark Zuckerberg, the founder of Facebook, has gained fame and fortune for his work.

(left) Thomas Edison was a prolific inventor. Nicknamed "The Wizard of Menlo Park," Edison was responsible for the first practical incandescent lightbulb, the phonograph, and a motion picture camera. He was born in 1847 in Ohio, and at an early age showed great interest in science. By the time of his death in 1931, Edison held more than 1,000 patents. Edison also created the world's first industrial research lab.

Influences on the United States

The United States is a nation of immigrants. English **colonists** settled on the Eastern shores in the 1600s, and in the 1700s, Spanish missionaries established communities in the Southwest. Today, immigrants continue to come from all over the world—especially from **Latin America** and Asia. Many important inventors came to the United States as immigrants. Alexander Graham Bell, who invented the telephone, came from Scotland. Vladimir Zworykin, called the "father of television," came to the United States from Russia. Nikola Tesla was a major contributor to commercial electricity and a renowned pioneer in electrical engineering. He was born in a Serbian village and moved to the United States when he was 35. Enrico Fermi was born in Italy and came to the United Sates after receiving the Nobel Prize in Physics. He was a major contributor to the development of the atomic bomb during World War II. The co-founder of Yahoo, Jerry Yang, came to the United States from Taiwan.

(above) The first space shuttle was launched in 1981 from the Kennedy Space Center in Florida. Thousands of visitors flocked to Florida to see space launches until the end of the space shuttle program in 2011.

(left) Today Americans listen to music through their portable music players, including the iPod. The iPod was an invention of Apple co-founder Steve Jobs and was first released to the public in October 2001.

5

Many faiths

Religion has always played an important role in the lives of Americans, and today about 80 percent of the U.S. population follows one of the major world religions.

Native Americans

Native Americans had their own religious practices and beliefs hundreds of years before colonists arrived. Each Native American culture had a different system of beliefs. Pueblo farmers of the American Southwest held special ceremonies to honor ancestors, the Sun, and forces of nature such as rain. Hunters of the plains and prairies expressed religious ideas with dances and rituals that are still honored by Native Americans today.

Seeking freedom

Many settlers came to American **colonies** in the 1600s so they could worship freely. Puritans and Pilgrims started English settlements in Massachusetts and Connecticut where they could freely practice their religion. English Roman Catholics started a colony in what is now the state of Maryland. Colonists in Rhode Island decided that their colony would have no official church. William Penn started a colony in Pennsylvania where people of different religious backgrounds would live together peacefully. The Dutch colonial settlement of New Amsterdam welcomed people of many religions, and the first Jewish settlers came to New Amsterdam in 1654.

Native Americans from hundreds of tribes across the country meet at the Gathering of Nations. This annual event is a time to share cultures, dance, sing, and to carry on sacred traditions. The Gathering of Nations is usually held in New Mexico, and it is the largest Pow Wow in North America.

Heritage of freedom

The Founders of the United States believed in freedom and equality. The Declaration of Independence states that all people are **equal** and that all people have the right to "life, liberty, and the pursuit of happiness." Religious freedom is a basic, fundamental principle, and it was guaranteed to all Americans in the First Amendment of the Bill of Rights in the United States Constitution.

Today, Americans practice many religions. Protestants and Catholics form the largest group with just over 75 percent. About 52 percent are Protestant, and about 24 percent are Catholic. Just over a million Americans are Jewish, and hundreds of thousands are Muslim, Hindu, or Buddhist.

(below) According to the Jewish faith, when boys turn 13 and girls turn 12 they become responsible for their actions and can lead prayer services. A celebration, known as a Bar Mitzvah for boys and Bat Mitzvah for girls, is held where the young person reads from the Torah in front of family and friends.

Small towns and villages in New England are often home to small Protestant churches like this one, each marked with its own steeple.

(above) In the Catholic faith, First Communion is an important event for boys and girls, and for their families. The children wear white clothing, and girls often wear a veil. First Communion is considered to be one of the steps leading to Confirmation, a tradition that is similar to the Jewish Bar Mitzvah.

Christian holidays

For Christians, the Christmas holiday marks the birth of Jesus Christ. The teachings of Jesus are holy to Christians. People celebrate Christmas with church services and with family gatherings. They exchange presents, have special meals, and listen to holiday music. Many Christians also give food, clothing, and money to help the needy. While people decorate their homes with lights and figures of Santa Claus and reindeer, they also decorate with evergreen trees and religious symbols such as nativities. Christmas, December 25, is a national holiday. Government offices and most businesses are closed on that day.

Easter is the most important spring holiday for Christians. It is usually in March or April. This holiday marks the death and resurrection, or rebirth, of Jesus Christ. Symbols of Easter include flowers, eggs, bunnies, and baby chicks. Many children receive baskets of candy at Easter.

(below) Christians often gather to worship together on Easter morning. The Hollywood Bowl in Los Angeles, California, is a traditional site for sunrise services, attracting Christians of all denominations.

For Christians, nativity scenes celebrate the birth of Jesus Christ in a manger, surrounded by his mother Mary, his father Joseph, the three Wise Men, and farm animals.

In neighborhoods throughout the country, families decorate their homes with lights to celebrate the Christmas holidays.

8

In the Muslim faith, it is common for men and women to cover their heads. Women wear a scarf while men wear a piece of cloth called a keffiyeh. Adults often read to children from the Koran during Ramadan.

Jewish holidays

The most important Jewish holidays celebrated in the United States are Passover, Rosh Hashanah, and Yom Kippur. Passover comes in the spring, and the other two holidays fall in September or October. Passover celebrates the end of slavery for Israelites in Egypt. People gather with friends and family to hold a special ceremonial meal called Seder. Rosh Hashanah marks the beginning of the new year on the Jewish calendar. Yom Kippur, known as the Day of Atonement, falls ten days later. It is the day when people ask for forgiveness. Jewish people traditionally observe Yom Kippur with fasting and prayer.

Muslim holidays

The month-long festival of Ramadan is the most important observance for Muslims. The time of Ramadan changes each year. During this month, healthy adults fast during daylight hours. They eat breakfast before sunrise and do not eat again until late evening. People share meals with family and friends. The last day of Ramadan is Eid ul-Fitr. On this day, friends and families gather, exchange gifts and cards, and give money to people who need their help.

Other religions, other celebrations

Many people from India in the United States celebrate Diwali, known as the festival of lights. For Hindus, Diwali is one of the most important festivals of the year. People light candles and oil lamps to welcome the Hindu goddess of wealth, Lakshmi.

Many Buddhists celebrate the new year in late winter or early spring. Later in the spring, Buddhists celebrate Buddha's birthday. In 2011, Buddhists marked Buddha's 2555th birthday! The teachings of Buddha are holy to Buddhists.

Women light candles to celebrate Diwali, the festival of light.

People in the United States enjoy many non-religious holiday celebrations. Some holidays, such as Thanksgiving, are national, official holidays. Others are celebrated locally or by certain groups of Americans.

National holidays

The first Memorial Day was observed in the 1860s to remember soldiers of the **Civil War.** Now Memorial Day is observed on the last Monday of May each year. The largest Memorial Day observances are held in Arlington National Cemetery outside Washington, D.C. About 5,000 people gather there on this day to remember those who lost their lives while serving in the United States military. In 2000, a law was passed to create a National Moment of Remembrance. This moment occurs at 3 p.m. local time on Memorial Day. People are asked to observe a moment of silence or to turn on their car headlights to show that they remember those who died.

On Memorial Day, family members and volunteer organizations decorate the tombstones of America's veterans with flags honoring those men and women who served in the military.

(above right) Every year thousands of people gather in the nation's capital to celebrate the Fourth of July. The festivities end with a magnificent fireworks display at the National Mall, between the Capitol and the Lincoln Memorial.

On July 4, 1776, the United States declared its independence from Great Britain. Americans celebrate the birthday of the United States of America on July 4 with picnics, parades, concerts, and especially with spectacular fireworks. Many cities hold parades and concerts featuring **patriotic** music. Musicians play *The Star-Spangled Banner, America The Beautiful,* and marching songs. The United States flag and its colors—red, white, and blue—are everywhere. In every city and town, large and small, people come together to celebrate the founding of the United States and the **ideals** of **liberty** and equality.

The first Monday in September marks the holiday known as Labor Day. This holiday honors working people all over the United States. Labor **unions** organized the first Labor

For decades, cities across the United States have celebrated working men and women with Labor Day parades featuring floats like the one shown here.

Day event in 1882. Unions wanted to show their importance as they began winning rights for workers, such as safer work places, better pay, and shorter workdays. Today, American towns and cities hold parades and festivals to honor working men and women. The Labor Day weekend also marks the end of summer and because the holiday falls on Monday, Americans are able to enjoy a three-day weekend.

Veterans Day, celebrated on November 11, was created in 1919 to mark the end of World War I. This holiday honors United States **veterans** of all wars. In 2010, there were nearly 22 million veterans in the United States. A national ceremony is held at 11 a.m. on November 11 at the Tomb of the Unknown Soldier in Arlington Cemetery to honor all the men and women who have served in the nation's armed forces.

(below) On the fourth Thursday of November, families sit down to celebrate Thanksgiving with a traditional dinner of turkey, stuffing, potatoes, and squash.

Held on the fourth Thursday in November, Thanksgiving is one of the most important holidays in the United States. Like Independence Day, it expresses the ideals of American culture. Symbols of Thanksgiving, such as children dressed as Pilgrims, come from a feast held in 1621 in Massachusetts. Pilgrims gathered to give thanks to God for guiding them safely to the New World. Native Americans were invited to join the Pilgrims, and the feast lasted for three days. The tradition of Thanksgiving, however, is even older. Native Americans and settlers in Newfoundland, Florida, Maine, and Virginia probably gave thanks at harvest festivals before 1621. In 1777, the Continental Congress provided the new nation with its first official proclamation of Thanksgiving. In 1789, George Washington, the first president of the United States, created the first Thanksgiving Day. Then, in 1863, during the Civil War, President Abraham Lincoln declared Thanksgiving a national holiday, to be celebrated on the final Thursday of every November. The date has been changed to the

(left) This memorial commemorates the 26,000 citizens of Washington, D.C., who served in the military during World War I. The monument was dedicated on Armistice Day in 1931.

fourth Thursday of the month, but Thanksgiving is still a time when families get together and give thanks for the things that they have. More people travel by train, bus, airplane, and car over the long Thanksgiving weekend than at any other time of the year. The traditional Thanksgiving meal includes turkey, sweet potatoes, cranberries, and pumpkin pie. These foods were new to the newly arrived Europeans, but they were native to North America.

Other holidays through the year

Many African Americans celebrate Kwanzaa, which was created in 1966 as a way to bring the African American community together. Kwanzaa celebrations begin on December 26 and end on January 1 with a feast. On each night of Kwanzaa a candle is lit in honor of one of seven principles related to building and reinforcing the sense of community.

The New Year celebration begins with a bang in many places! Parties and festivals take place all over the United States on December 31. At midnight, as the new year begins, people cheer and watch fireworks. In New York City's Times Square, thousands gather to watch as a giant

Ron Karenga is known as the creator of Kwanzaa. He is shown here (center) celebrating Kwanzaa with his family and friends.

illuminated ball drops to signal the start of the new year. Some people make **resolutions** for the new year. Many cities hold parades on January 1, celebrating the new year, and college football bowl games are often held on New Year's Day.

People in China, Korea, Japan, Vietnam, and other parts of Asia celebrate a **lunar** new year in late January or in February. Lunar new year celebrations are held in the United States, too.

This festive dragon is paraded through the streets of Chinatown in Los Angeles, California, to celebrate the Chinese New Year.

(left) The tradition of dropping a ball from the flagpole in New York City's Times Square began on December 31, 1907. Today the ball, currently made of Waterford crystal, descends 77 feet (23 m) in one minute. More than one million people gather in Times Square to watch, and another 70 million watch the event over video or on television.

Cities with large Asian populations hold parades with paper dragons, dancers, and drumming to mark the new year.

In Louisiana, early spring brings Mardi Gras, a festival marked with special meals, parties, and a huge parade. People in New Orleans spend the year making elaborate floats and costumes for Mardi Gras, a festival that grew out of the French Catholic heritage of Louisiana.

Cinco de Mayo, May 5, is the date of a Mexican military victory. Mexican-Americans in Texas, California, Arizona, and New Mexico celebrate their heritage on this day with parades and festivals. The world's largest Cinco de Mayo festival is held in California.

On the third Monday in January, Americans honor the **legacy** of Reverend Martin Luther King, Jr., who became a national hero during the civil rights struggle. He and his followers used **nonviolent** methods of protest to fight inequality. Dr. King was a great speaker who motivated people to work together and take risks to change unjust laws. Americans honor the work of Dr. King by spending the day helping the less fortunate. Many cities organize parades to remind us of his efforts to gain equality for people of all races and ethnicities.

César Chávez was inspired by the example of Martin Luther King, Jr. Chávez also used nonviolent methods to win fair pay and safer working conditions for farm workers. His birthday, March 31, is observed in many states. Each year, Americans honor King and Chávez by doing **volunteer** work in their communities. They may sort donated clothing and books, make blankets and scarves for homeless people, or put together activity kits for children in emergency shelters.

(above) Martin Luther King, Jr. won many awards for his work, including the Nobel Peace Prize and the Presidential Medal of Freedom he is holding here.

(left) Wearing traditional costumes, these dancers celebrate Cinco de Mayo. People also celebrate this day by eating traditional Mexican foods.

13

American music combines influences from Native Americans, West Africa, Europe, Mexico, and South America. People have come to the United States from nearly every corner of the earth, bringing songs, musical instruments, and new ways of playing music.

Spirituals and gospel

People forced into slavery brought musical traditions from their homes in Africa. Singing brought comfort and made work a little easier in the Americas. Singing was also a way to worship. Whether they were singing in joy or in sorrow, enslaved people used rhythms, tones, and harmonies from Africa. Over time, this music became **gospel music,** blues, rhythm and blues, and **jazz.** Performers such as Louis Armstrong and Ray Charles brought these musical styles to people throughout the United States and all over the world.

(below) Gospel music is a major part of many church services as people joyfully celebrate with their voices.

During the 1920s, 1930s, and 1940s, jazz was king, and no one did big-band jazz better than Duke Ellington and his orchestra. A talented pianist, Ellington was also a composer and wrote thousands of songs, including several motion-picture scores.

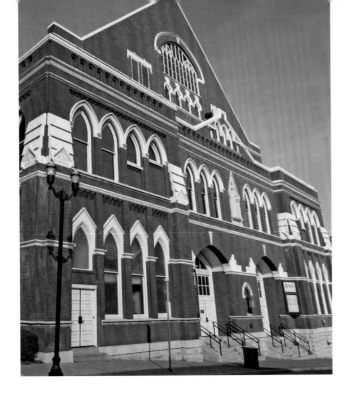

(left) *The Ryman Auditorium in Nashville, Tennessee, was home of the Grand Ole Opry from 1943 to 1974. The building has been designated a National Historic Landmark.*

American composers

George Gershwin and Aaron Copland were both born in Brooklyn, New York. Gershwin was inspired by spirituals and jazz; Copland was inspired by the music of the Appalachians and the West. Both wrote classical **orchestral** music. Richard Rodgers, another New York composer, explored the heritage of American music through musicals. Working with different **lyricists,** including Oscar Hammerstein, Rodgers wrote music for live theater and movies, creating tunes that are now as familiar as folk music.

Country and bluegrass

Immigrants from England, Ireland, and Scotland faced great hardships in the Appalachian Mountains. They expressed joy and sorrow through the rhythms and harmonies of their ancestors. When *Grand Ole Opry,* a radio program from Nashville, Tennessee, broadcast this music, people all over the United States started to love country music. Hank Williams, June Carter, and Johnny Cash are some of the many performers who brought this music to the world. Today, country music has many styles. Bluegrass is a form that uses only **acoustic** instruments.

(below) Country singer Dolly Parton sings at the Grand Ole Opry in Nashville, Tennessee.

The music for the movie State Fair was written by Rodgers and Hammerstein in 1945, and it was the one time when the two men wrote music only for a film. The movie and its music was a gigantic hit, another success for the pair of composers.

15

(left) Elvis Presley's career took off when he was in his teens, and he quickly vaulted to success. He was nominated for 14 Grammy Awards and won the award three times. He has sold over 1 billion records throughout the world, and he starred in 33 successful films as well.

Rock 'n' roll is here to stay

In the 1950s, record producers mixed African American rhythm and blues styles with traditional country music. The result was rock and roll, and it gave American teenagers a music of their own. Elvis Presley was the king of rock 'n' roll. Along with performers such as Chuck Berry and Buddy Holly, Elvis influenced musicians in other countries, especially in England. Like other musical forms, rock 'n' roll has changed with the times. Michael Jackson in the 1980s and more recently Lady Gaga have carried rock 'n' roll into the present. Soul music, disco, punk, hip-hop, and rap all have at least some roots in rock 'n' roll.

(top right) Lady Gaga gained fame in 2008 with her album The Fame. *The album won six Grammy nominations. She has been nominated for 12 Grammy Awards and won six. Forbes Magazine has also listed her as one of the world's "most powerful women."*

Queen Latifah was born Dana Elaine Owens. She is a successful singer, rapper, and actress. She has been nominated for seven Grammy Awards and has won one. She has also been nominated for Emmy and Academy Awards.

Hip-hop and rap

In the 1970s, Grandmaster Flash used turntables and electronic equipment to pioneer a new musical sound. Performers such as Run-DMC, Queen Latifah, and Lauryn Hill have been among those who have carried the hip-hop message to the United States and the world. Hip-hop music uses emcees or deejays to mix recorded music, distinctive rhythms, and spoken word (rap) to convey an urban culture based in primarily Latino and African American neighborhoods of large American cities.

American art

Painting

Until the time of the American Revolution, people living in the colonies thought of themselves as British. They made furniture, clothing, and houses in English and European styles. Yet few people in the colonies were able to study art and become as skilled as European painters. John Singleton Copley was probably the first great American painter. His portraits captured many leaders of the American Revolution.

After the nation gained its independence, a group of American painters wanted to express the growing power of their new nation. This group became known as the Hudson River school. Thomas Cole, who was born in England and came to the United States as a teenager; his student Frederic Church; and other artists painted New York's Hudson River Valley. Beautiful flowers, craggy mountains, and powerful waterfalls portrayed a new and complex American character.

(above) Copley painted this portrait of Paul Revere in 1768. Although Revere was active in colonial revolutionary efforts at this time, Copley painted him with a silver object, showing his occupation as a silversmith.

(below) In the 1907 painting Cavalry Charge on the Southern Plains, *Frederic Remington captures the energy of mounted troops as they gallop off to battle.*

American artists recorded the push to the West as well. Albert Bierstadt, whose family came to the United States when he was three years old, saw grandeur in the vast **landscapes**. George Catlin portrayed Native Americans and also wrote about the loss of their lands and the destruction of their culture. Frederic Remington captured the lives of cowhands, western towns, and Native Americans in **illustrations** for magazines and newspapers. His paintings and sculpture of western life influenced popular views and much later, movies about the West.

In the 1900s, painters found new ways to portray changes in United States culture. **Abstract** artists worked with color, shape, and texture to express emotions and ideas. Jackson Pollock, Lee Krasner, Helen Frankenthaler, Alma Woodsey Thomas, and Frank Stella are among the most important American abstract painters. Other artists portrayed people and objects, but the objects they chose and how they presented them were new. Jacob Lawrence and Romare Bearden depicted African American culture and history with strong graphic images. Roy Lichtenstein's paintings looked like comic book pictures. Georgia O'Keeffe painted huge flowers and desert landscapes. They are just some of the artists who changed the way Americans saw their nation and their times.

Photography

In the early 1900s, Alfred Stieglitz decided that photographs could be art, just like paintings. Ansel Adams controlled the exposure in his photographs to capture nature with startling clarity. Dorothea Lange used her camera to document the human suffering of the Great Depression. As photography grew more important, photographers found new ways to use it. Gordon Parks put pictures of the civil rights movement on the front pages and covers of newspapers and magazines. Cindy Sherman dressed up as characters from movies and television and took pictures of herself to comment on ways women are portrayed in American culture.

(above) Ansel Adams was both a photographer and an artist. In this photo, he captured the beauty of the Teton mountain range and Snake River in Wyoming.

(left) Although he is better known for his painting, Roy Lichtenstein created this mosaic, named The Head, *for the 1992 Summer Olympics held in Barcelona, Spain. It was his first outdoor work using ceramic tile.*

Sculpture

Sculpture is three-dimensional art made of stone, metal, or other material. In the 1800s, Daniel Chester French created inspiring public statues. He is especially known for his massive statue of Abraham Lincoln in the Lincoln Memorial in Washington, D.C. In the mid- to late-1900s, George Segal, a sculptor associated with **Pop Art,** used plaster bandages to make life-sized sculptures of everyday people. Their faces were intentionally unrecognizable, giving them a ghost-like quality. During this same time period, the abstract sculptor Alexander Calder created colorful mobiles and other works with moving parts. Louise Nevelson made large detailed sculptures, often all black or all white. Sculptor Richard Serra is known for huge metal structures that seem to change as the viewer walks around or through them.

(right) Alexander Calder is known for his delicately balanced mobiles, often created on a grand scale.

(below) George Segal created this moving image of men waiting in a bread line during the Great Depression for the Franklin D. Roosevelt Memorial in Washington, D.C. The memorial was dedicated in 1997 by President Bill Clinton.

American architecture

Colonial architects and builders were influenced by European building styles. Thomas Jefferson, third President of the United States, liked the columns and domes of Italian architecture. Jefferson's designs for his home, Monticello, and the buildings of the University of Virginia, show this influence. Many churches, synagogues, and Roman Catholic cathedrals built in the 1800s used domes, **columns,** and other features taken from ancient Greece and Rome, places where **democracy** and **republican** forms of government began. Charles Bulfinch used these neoclassical designs in the Massachusetts State House and other buildings.

Other American buildings, especially universities and public buildings, used European Gothic styles. These buildings were usually made of stone, and they had tall towers and pointed windows. As American cities grew, architects turned to designing outdoor spaces as well. Frederick Law Olmsted designed Central Park in New York City to give people places to enjoy the outdoors. He also designed other parks in New York, Boston, and other cities. John A. Roebling, a German-born American civil engineer, designed important bridges, including New York City's Brooklyn Bridge.

Massachusetts State House, Boston, Massachusetts, designed by Charles Bulfinch

(below) St. Patrick's Cathedral, New York City

The Smithsonian Institution Building, also known as The Castle, in Washington D.C.

a California architect and one of the first women architects, had a similar view. She was known for creating beautiful buildings out of local materials that fit into the hilly landscapes of the San Francisco Bay area. Her most famous building was a sprawling mansion designed for newspaper owner William Randolph Hearst.

(left) Hearst Castle was designed by Julia Morgan for wealthy newspaper magnate William Randolph Hearst. Overlooking the Pacific Ocean, the home is located halfway between Los Angeles and San Francisco, California. Morgan worked on the home, its outbuildings, and gardens for 28 years.

Designed by Frank Lloyd Wright for a wealthy Pittsburgh family, Fallingwater was partially built over a waterfall. It is a National Historic Landmark, and in 1991 the house was named the best all-time work of American architecture.

Modern architecture

In the late 1800s, American cities were growing rapidly and becoming more and more crowded. People had to find housing, but there was no room to spread out within city limits. Thanks to electricity and elevators, people could build taller buildings to fit more people and offices in less land. Louis H. Sullivan was a pioneer in the design of skyscrapers. His motto was "Form follows function," which means that the design of a building should match the building's purpose. One of Sullivan's assistants was a young man named Frank Lloyd Wright. Wright became the leading name among a group of architects called the Prairie School, and he is still one of the nation's most famous architects. Wright wanted to create buildings that would blend with the **environment** and serve the people who would use them. Julia Morgan,

English-speaking settlers in Virginia, Massachusetts, and the other original thirteen colonies brought their language to the United States. American English, however, is different from British English. American English has been influenced by the languages of Native Americans; of African slaves; and of German, Swedish, Irish, French, and Spanish-speaking immigrants. For a long time, there were no rules about spelling American English words. Noah Webster changed that when he published the first dictionary of American English in 1828.

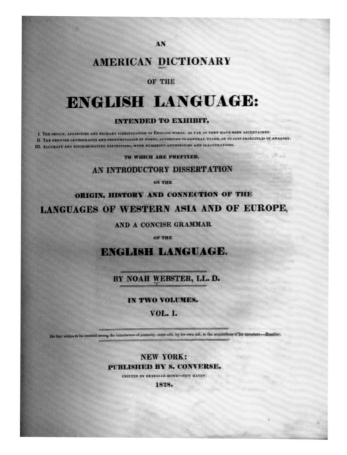

Noah Webster compiled the first American dictionary of the English language in 1806. He immediately went to work on a new edition, which was published in 1828. This new edition contained 70,000 entries. He added words that were new to English, such as skunk and chowder. He also simplified spellings, for example, changing plough to plow.

Other languages

American English continues to change. Most immigrants to the United States learn English, and they bring words and phrases that influence the English language. At the same time, some young people are learning the languages of their ancestors. People of Native American nations such as the Ojibwe, the Dakota, and the Walla Walla are working to preserve their traditional languages. Innovation brings its own vocabulary, too, and the vocabulary used in emerging technology continues to grow.

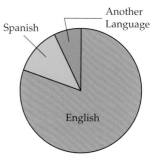

Languages Spoken at Home by Americans

Spanish
Another Language
English

Ages 5 or older; 2007 data
Source: United States Census

| COMMON ENGLISH WORDS AND THEIR ROOTS ||
Word	Origin
alligator	Spanish
blink	Dutch
boomerang	Australia
caddy	Scotland
canyon	Spanish
cot	Hindi or Urdu
coyote	Spanish
croquet	French
dam	Dutch
hurricane	Spanish
ketchup	China
plaid	Scotland
renegade	Spanish
silk	China
thug	Hindi or Urdu
tweed	Scotland

Americans have always been great storytellers. Some stories are funny, some are sad, and others offer examples of courage and hard work. Rip Van Winkle, Paul Bunyan, and Brer Rabbit are imaginary characters. Stories about Johnny Appleseed, Annie Oakley, John Henry, Betsy Ross, Davy Crockett, and Pocahontas are based on real people or real events. Whether based on real or made-up people, these stories are part of the fabric of American culture. One episode of the legend of Paul Bunyan appears below.

Paul Bunyan

Legend says that when Paul Bunyan was a baby in Maine he rolled over in his sleep and destroyed three acres of woods! His father built him a floating cradle. Every time baby Paul rolled around in his cradle he caused a sixty-foot (18-meter) tide. Paul was raised on moose milk, and he logged most of the forests in Maine while he was still a little boy. "That kid's going to be a great logger," his father said.

Paul would never let anyone measure him, but when he was fourteen, old Pete Curry, who was seven feet nine inches in his socks, came up only to Paul's kneecap. Of course, Paul hadn't reached his full height at that point.

Paul was strong, but he was gentle. Most of the time his voice was as gentle as a mother's singing her baby to sleep. But when he was angry, he could shout so loud that he would shake leaves off the trees for miles around.

Paul had a blue ox named Babe who was so strong he could straighten a crooked road. It took three-quarters of the grain grown in Iowa to feed that ox, and once, when Babe was thirsty, he sucked a river dry. Some people say Paul Bunyan dug out the Great Lakes so Babe would have water to drink. From Michigan, Paul went to Wisconsin, the Great North Woods of Minnesota, to Oregon, and then to Washington. If you're looking for Paul now, you should look in Alaska, but your eyes better be good. Paul moves pretty fast!

BEMIDJI

PAUL BUNYAN 1937

Americans love hearing poems and stories told aloud, and they like reading them. In the mid-1700s, however, not all Americans could read, especially those living in the Middle and Southern colonies. Many children had to work instead of going to school. One hundred years after the nation was founded, only about two out of every hundred adults graduated from high school. Even so, books were valued and important.

Poetry

Anne Bradstreet, who wrote in the 1600s, is considered America's first poet. Many of America's greatest poems, however, were written in the late 1800s and early 1900s. Walt Whitman wrote poems about the grief of the nation after the Civil War and about city life. Emily Dickinson wrote poems you may have read. "I'm nobody! Who are you?/Are you nobody, too?" are the first two lines from one of her most famous poems. Edna St. Vincent Millay was one of many young writers and artists who flocked to New York City in the early 1900s. Robert Frost, a New Englander, wrote beloved poems such as "The Road Not Taken" and "Stopping by Woods on a Snowy Evening." Carl Sandburg wrote poems about life in the Midwest and the booming city of Chicago. Langston Hughes carried poetry into modern times using the rhythms of blues and jazz in poems such as "Harlem" and "Dream Variations." More recently, Robert Pinsky served as Poet Laureate of the United States for three terms, and readers young and old enjoy the poems of African American poets Nikki Giovanni, Gwendolyn Brooks, and Maya Angelou.

(left) Emily Dickinson lived in near seclusion in Amherst, Massachusetts, for her entire life. Her poems were not published until several years after her death in 1886.

(below) Robert Frost was born in San Francisco, California, but moved to New England when he was 11. His poetry revolves around the lives of New Englanders and their landscape.

Early American novels and short stories

Benjamin Franklin was an inventor, a statesman, and a publisher in the 1700s. He also wrote many popular books, political **essays,** humorous stories, and the story of his own life. His *Poor Richard's Almanack* was a favorite because of its information, advice, and humorous, short, well-known sayings called proverbs.

Washington Irving was the first big name in American literature. His stories "Rip Van Winkle" and "The Legend of Sleepy Hollow" were published in 1819, but they took place before the American Revolution. Edgar Allan Poe, who some people say invented detective fiction and **science fiction**, began to publish dark, scary stories in the 1830s. Herman Melville wrote adventure stories set at sea. His most famous book, *Moby Dick*, was about a huge white whale, and some consider it to be the greatest American novel ever written.

(below) In this scene from the movie Little Women *based on the novel by Louisa May Alcott, the family gathers to read a letter from their father who is away with the troops during the Civil War.*

The Civil War and beyond

Harriet Beecher Stowe's novel *Uncle Tom's Cabin* made people see the **injustice** of slavery. A few years after the book was published, the Civil War (1861–1865) changed the United States in many ways and slavery became illegal.

Following the Civil War, more and more people moved to cities and worked in factories. Writers tried to describe every part of American life during these changing times. Louisa May Alcott wrote *Little Women* and other books for children and adults. Mark Twain wrote about boys growing up along the Mississippi River in *The Adventures of Tom Sawyer* and *Huckleberry Finn*. In the early 1900s, Willa Cather described life on the prairie in her novels *My Antonia* and *O! Pioneers*. Many magazines started or grew in the late 1800s and early 1900s. Exciting stories, articles, and pictures came in the mail every month or even every week.

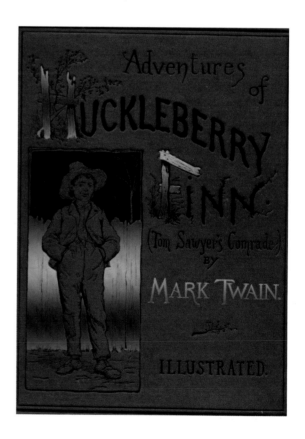

Huckleberry Finn *was first published in the United States in 1885. Although the novel has raised some controversy because of its language, it is considered to be one of the great American novels.*

Today, Americans from many ethnic groups write books for all readers. Toni Morrison was the first African American to win the **Nobel Prize** in literature. Amy Tan writes books based on stories of her Chinese ancestors for children and adults, and Linda Sue Park writes about children from Korean history and in the United States. Louise Erdrich and Sherman Alexie write stories of Native Americans in the United States today, and Sandra Cisneros and Gary Soto are Mexican-American authors who write for children and teenagers. Julia Alvarez writes from her experiences as an immigrant from the Dominican Republic.

Science fiction and fantasy

Some of the world's favorite science fiction writers have been Americans. Isaac Asimov, Ray Bradbury, Madeleine L'Engle, and Ursula K. Le Guin are all great writers of science fiction and fantasy. The first title in a very popular American fantasy series appeared in 1900. It was called *The Wonderful Wizard of Oz*. Children who read the book were so enchanted by the imaginary world of Oz that they wrote to L. Frank Baum, the author, and asked him how they might get there.

Toni Morrison

(below) Amy Tan

Julia Alvarez

27

The Little House on the Prairie books by Laura Ingalls Wilder was made into a popular television series that ran for nine seasons, and viewers can still see re-runs of the television shows. The books were also the basis for a five-hour television mini-series, several made-for-television movies, and a live theater show.

Children's books

Children love to read fantasy, but they also love adventure. Laura Ingalls Wilder wrote the beloved *Little House on the Prairie* series, which are books about a family settling on the frontier. Another great American writer was Theodore Seuss Geisel. Writing as Dr. Seuss, his stories about the Cat in the Hat, the Grinch, Green Eggs and Ham, and lots of other funny rhymes and silly pictures made books fun for millions of children who were learning to read. Other beloved children's authors include Jan Brett, whose complex artwork and simple stories attract and charm readers of all ages. Brett has won many awards for her work. Beautifully illustrated titles such as *Berlioz the Bear, The Mitten,* and *The Umbrella* have all won individual awards for best children's books. Each new Brett book is eagerly anticipated by her fans. Maurice Sendak gained fame in the United States and around the world for his book *Where the Wild Things Are.* Like Brett, Sendak has won numerous awards, including the Caldecott and the National Medal of Arts.

New ways to read

In the late 1900s and early 2000s, the way many Americans read changed. People bought more books via the Internet, and people began to read eBooks on computers. Hundreds of books, magazines, and newspapers can now be read on an eReader, which weighs less than a single small book. Books and magazines are no longer the only form of reading, either. More people read blogs and keep up through **social media** such as Facebook and Twitter.

Television

Although television was invented much earlier, it wasn't until the 1950s that large numbers of American households had a television set. At first, there were only three TV channels. In the 1950s and 1960s, many American families tuned in to watch **variety shows,** comedies, sports events, game shows, and television dramas. *I Love Lucy* with Lucille Ball and Desi Arnaz was a popular comedy. Americans also watched television to get the news.

The 1960s brought color television and the groundbreaking show *Sesame Street*. In 1969, Americans watched the first moon landing on television. As television became more popular, television advertising also became more important. Television ads influenced what Americans bought and the way they talked and joked. The number of stations increased to the hundreds. By the end of the 1960s, American television shows could be seen around the world. Today, with the advent of cable television, Americans can choose from hundreds of stations and programs for every interest. TV shows are also available on DVDs and online.

Americans watched spellbound when American astronauts first landed on the moon in 1969. Putting a man and a flag on the moon were extraordinary events watched worldwide.

(below) The Muppets are a beloved group of puppets designed by Jim Henson. This cast of talented puppets has been on television, in the movies, and even in live theater productions.

Meryl Streep is one of the most talented and respected actors working today. She has received 17 Academy Award nominations and won for Kramer vs. Kramer, Sophie's Choice, and in 2012, for her role in the movie The Iron Lady. In the film Streep portrays Margaret Thatcher, who served as Britain's Prime Minister from 1979 to 1990.

Hollywood and movies

Film production companies based in Hollywood, California, make movies that are shown throughout the United States and around the world. Although Americans enjoy going to theaters to see movies on large screens, people now watch movies on television sets; computers; and on hand-held devices such as smartphones and portable media players. Some of the most popular recent Hollywood films have been directed by George Lucas, Ron Howard, and Steven Spielberg. George Lucas is known for the special effects in his *Star Wars* movies. Ron Howard was acting on television when he was six. He grew up to direct popular dramas, **thrillers,** and comedies. Two of his famous movies are *Apollo 13* and *Cocoon*. Steven Spielberg is a versatile director of science fiction, adventure, and dramatic films. Two of his films are *E.T.* and *The Adventures of Tin-Tin*.

Great actors

Glitz and glitter! You can see all the stars at the **Academy Awards.** The performers, writers, directors, composers, and all the other people who work to make movies that make audiences laugh, cry, and sit on the edge of their seats gather in Hollywood to see who will win the gold statue called an Oscar. Tom Hanks, Denzel Washington, Jennifer Hudson, Meryl Streep, Halle Berry, George Clooney, and Angelina Jolie are some of the actors who have walked away with awards. Do you wonder who will win this year?

E.T., directed by Steven Spielberg, was a blockbuster movie and a science fiction classic that captured the minds and imaginations of Americans young and old.

Animation

Walt Disney was one of nation's most famous filmmakers. Disney created his own actors—Mickey Mouse and Donald Duck—and turned fairy tales and folktales into animated films such as *Snow White, Beauty and the Beast,* and *Cinderella.* These and other Disney films became some of the most viewed movies in the world. Disney used the money he made from his films to build theme parks in California and Florida. Tourists from all over the United States and the world visit these parks to see the characters and settings of Disney films "in person."

Minnie Mouse, Mickey Mouse, and other Disney characters have starred in movies, and are on hand to greet visitors at the Disney studios and at the Disney theme parks in Florida and California.

A new way to animate

In 1995, the first feature-length animated film made with computers was released. *Toy Story,* which featured the voices of Tom Hanks and Tim Allen, was a hit, and it changed the way films were made. *Toy Story* is considered by many film critics to be one of the most revolutionary movies in the history of animation. Pixar, the company that made the film, went on to make *Finding Nemo, Up,* and of course, more *Toy Story* movies. In 2006, Pixar became part of the Disney company. This entertainment powerhouse continues to make successful animated movies. In 2011, Steven Spielberg directed the award-winning animated film *The Adventures of Tin-Tin: The Secret Unicorn.* It was Spielberg's first animated film. John Williams, who wrote the musical scores for *E.T.,* the *Star Wars* saga, and three Harry Potter movies, wrote the score for *Tin-Tin.*

(below) The Pixar/Disney movie Up *received five Academy Award nominations and won awards for best animated film and best original score. The El Capitan Theatre, a landmark building in Hollywood, first opened in 1926 and is now operated by the Disney Company.*

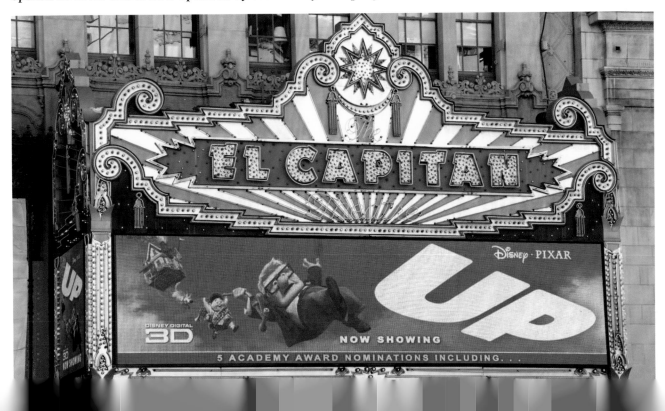

Glossary

abstract Dealing with concepts, not a true pictorial representation

Academy Awards Important prizes given each year to movies and people who work in the film industry

acoustic An instrument whose sound is not changed or made bigger by electronics

Civil War A war between the northern and southern states of America over the role of slavery. The war began in 1861 and ended in 1865 with a victory for the North and the abolishment of slavery.

colonists People who settle new land and claim it for the government of another country

colonies Areas controlled by a distant country

columns Tall posts or pillars that are used to help hold up a building

democracy A form of government in which people choose their leaders and participate in making laws through an election process

environment The living things and conditions of a place

equal Being treated exactly the same as everyone else

essays Short pieces of writing written from a personal point of view

gospel music Songs whose lyrics have a relationship with the Bible

ideals Beliefs about what is right or just

illustrations Pictures that are made to help explain a story

injustice An action that is unfair

inventors People who design or create something new

jazz American music with a lively rhythm that came from ragtime and blues

landscapes Pictures that show a view of natural scenery

Latin America Mexico, Central, and South America

legacy Things that are passed on from another person or from a person's actions

liberty Freedom

lunar Relating to the Moon

lyricist Person who writes words for a song

Nobel Prize A special award given each year to a person or a group for working in a particular area, such as writing

nonviolent Acting in a peaceful manner

orchestral Refers to music composed for an orchestra, a group of people who play music together

patriotic Showing love for one's country

Pop Art A 1960s art movement that presented everyday objects and scenes in nontraditional ways

prolific Producing a large amount

republican Refers to a form of government in which the people elect representatives who make the laws

resolutions Things a person decides and promises to do

science fiction Made-up stories and movies based on science or technology of the future

social media Ways in which people communicate and exchange information electronically, online, or through websites

thrillers Stories or movies that have a lot of suspense or exciting action

Torah A Jewish holy book

unions Organizations that form to fight for improvement of working conditions, wages, and benefits

variety shows Programs that feature different kinds of entertainment, including singing, dancing, and comedy

veterans People who have fought in a war for their country

volunteer Offering to work for no money; a person who offers to work for no money

Index

Academy Awards 31
Adventures of Tom Sawyer, The 26
American architecture 20–21
American Revolution 17

Benjamin Franklin 26
Bill of Rights
    First Amendment 7
Civil war 10, 11, 25, 26

Duke Ellington 14

Elvis Presley 16
Equality 7, 10, 13

Facebook 4, 28

Frank Lloyd Wright 21

George Segal 19
George Washington 11
Gordon Parks 18
Gospel music 14
Great Depression 18, 19
Great North Woods 24

Hearst Castle 21
Hudson River 17

Innovation 4, 22
Internet 4, 28, 29

Kennedy Space Center 5

Labor unions 10

Mark Twain 26
Native Americans 6, 11, 14, 18
New Amsterdam settlement 6
Noah Webster 22

Pop Art 19
Protestant churches 6

Robert Frost 25
Science fiction 26, 27, 30
Sculpture 18, 19
Summer Olympics 18

Technology 4
Thomas Edison 4
Twitter 28

United States
    composers 15, 31
    culture 4
    Declaration of
        Independence 7
    holidays 9, 10, 11, 12, 13
    immigrants 5, 15, 22
    languages 22
    religion 4, 6, 7, 8, 9

Walt Disney 31
Wonderful Wizard of Oz, The 27
World War I 11
World War II 5